Werner Bischof spent nearly two years in Japan collecting material for this book. He was also at that time, 1951-52, reporting photographically on the Korean War. It is remarkable that with fresh impressions of killing and death in his eyes he could focus so clearly and with so much humanity on the beauty and dignity of Japan. The introductory text is written by Robert Guillain, Far East correspondent of the world-famous Paris newspaper "Le Monde."

1 Shinto priests crossing a courtyard of the Meiji Temple in Tokyo. Snow is falling on the pine-trees and the cloisters and on their paper umbrellas. This is Japan as it was a thousand years ago.

JAPAN BY WERNER BISCHOF
WITH TEXT BY ROBERT GUILLAIN
A GALLERY EDITION/BANTAM BOOKS/NEW YORK

*JAPAN / Bantam Gallery Edition / Published November 1961.
All rights reserved. Copyright © Magnum Photos, Inc., 1961.
Published simultaneously in the United States and Canada. Bantam
Books are published by Bantam Books, Inc. Its trade-mark,
consisting of the words "Bantam Books" and the portrayal of a
bantam, is registered in the United States Patent Office and in other
countries. Marca Registrada. Printed in the United States of America. Bantam Books, Inc., 271 Madison Ave., New York 16, N. Y.*

JAPAN

JAPAN / BY ROBERT GUILLAIN

Although Japan lies on the far side of the globe, it is now just next door. The air journey from London to Tokyo takes no more than thirty-six hours, and soon it will take less. If you leave England on Sunday morning, by Monday evening (Greenwich Time) you can see Fujiyama—in the light of dawn, for the time of day will be different in the Country of the Rising Sun. In the modern world, distance has ceased to exist, except in the form of what one might call "economic distance," that is the price of the air passage.

The time has now come when, if he can afford the fare, a man no longer has the right to go through life without ever having seen the Imperial Palace in Tokyo or the Kyoto Temples. The temptation to make the journey is now greater than ever; Japan is one of the last countries to remain open to us in the whole of the Far East; almost the only one in which the Westerner can still travel to the most out-of-the-way places in peace and comfort.

If you open this book and look through the glimpses of Japan assembled with such delight by that great artist Werner Bischof shortly before his tragic death, you will see an astonishing world—for us, an unknown world—reflected as in a mirror. Unknown it should no longer be, just as it should no longer appear remote. We Europeans have lagged behind in the discovery, or re-discovery, of Japan since the end of her military adventure. The Americans are far ahead of us; their post-war occupation has made them familiar with all aspects of life in the green isles. They are far more keenly aware than we are that, in our shrunken world, Tokyo is one of the half-dozen places which are worthy of continuous attention.

By a curious phenomenon of reaction, America is even beginning to feel the influence of Japanese civilisation. American designers and architects have found inspiration in the highly idiomatic style of Japanese houses. The art treasures of Kyoto and Nara are put on show at San Francisco and New York, and the Kabuki Theatrical Company has appeared on Broadway. The world is going back to Japan, and Japan is coming back into the world. Are we to behave towards her like ignorant provincials, we Europeans who are better qualified than anyone else to understand certain aspects of her message and to appreciate her beauty?

In the year 1000 A.D., a Japanese poetess named Sei Shonagon wrote some delicious *Pillow-Sketches*, which included a list of "Things which make the heart beat faster". I could try to draw up a similar list for our own time (not to mention the list of "Things that are better forgotten", which would be quite a different matter). It would be a long list, and yet, however long I made it, it would still lack that elusive quality which, once he has felt, binds the Western visitor so strongly to Japan.

The charm does not always work. A minority of Westerners remain untouched and hostile. But the others, who come under the spell, are unable to explain what has happened. Some magic wand has been waved or some habit-forming drug imbibed. One can be homesick for Japan in a very special way. The memory of the country's darker aspects quickly fades, and its pleasant features grow still brighter in retrospect. The Westerner who has once made the country his home for any length of time is inconsolable, if he cannot go back; he is like someone who has been to Tahiti.

However, without seeking to imitate the style of the poetess of old, let me try to compile a list of the "Things which will make me go back to Japan".

I will go back—to put it at its lowest—to see Japan without the Japanese, that is for the sake of the country's very individual local colour; for the astonishment of seeing the originals of those images of nature that the deft brushes of the Nipponese artists have painted on silk; for the pine-tree with its twisted branches, the flight of the wild geese over Tokyo Bay, and the thatched villages in the misty valley at the foot of Fujiyama; for the blending of mountain and sea, and to watch the smoking volcanoes; for an island off Tokyo, which is a basket of red camelias floating on the edge of the Pacific.

I will go back to taste the joys of the tourist, not in European hotels, of course, but in the old, traditional inns —and in the fine weather, too, between March and November, because Japanese inns have no heating.

I will go back to enjoy the strange Japanese way of

life, the nudity of its comfort, its simplification of existence and its search for contentment in frugality and closeness to nature.

I will go back for the sake of the children, who are like live dolls; for the girls with their laughter, their Mongol eyelids, their brilliant black hair, their bare feet in wooden sandals and the pure metal of their hearts ensheathed in softness; for Japanese women, who seem to belong to a race different from that of the men, and are the country's finest achievement.

I will go back to see Tokyo by night, when its ugliness is transformed into a fairylike pattern; for the ancient town of Kyoto which is, with Paris, Rome and Pekin, one of the few towns in the world where the breath of the spirit can be felt; for the plays of the Nô theatre, each of which is a plunge into the depths of the past; for the old palace of Katsura, whose architects seem to have devined the secrets of Le Corbusier's art.

I will go back to assure myself that the West can learn certain lessons from the East; I will go back, so that Japan may teach me the refinements of the artistic sense and the gift of communing intensely with the mystery of nature; to reacquire from the Japanese that respect for the past, and the people of the past, that we Westerners have lost; to confirm that no one knows what politeness is until he has experienced Japanese politeness.

I will go back to savour the extreme peculiarities of the country and to discover, at the same time, that all the paths of civilisation, even the most winding, lead back in the end to man.

A word of warning, however; the initial contact is disappointing, misleading, even, for those who trust to first impressions. One ought to begin at Kyoto, but one lands at Tokyo. Unpleasant surprises occur thick and fast. The crowd seems an ugly herd of people. The immense suburbs are sad and dirty. The capital is a monstrous untidy village. Traditional Japan seems to have disappeared under the haphazard onslaughts of modern technique.

Escape immediately in the direction of the Fuji lakes or the temples of the Nikko Forest; then you will realize at once that Tokyo is not Japan, and you will learn to appreciate the rewards that await you, if you know how to make your discoveries patiently.

The first impact has at least the advantage of making the visitor see how different the country is from the conventional pictures of it that have been spread abroad. Where are the little doll-like Japanese women, bewigged and simpering, the men with their artificial grins, the paper houses, the miniature landscapes, and the so-called country of tiny people? Not to be seen! How far behind the times are we when we think of Japan in terms of Pierre Loti or even of Lafcadio Hearn? Their insipid, rose-coloured Japan has hindered understanding of the real Japan.

Real Japan is not rose-coloured; it is not all cherry-blossom. It is often sombre; the blossom and the flowers are often rare, and life cruel for the weak. A people with vitality coursing through their veins cannot give way to soft emotionalism; forty millions of them out of ninety-five millions are under twenty, and competition is very fierce. Can a country of earthquakes, tidal waves and volcanoes be insipid?

To the visitor's surprise, real Japan is lusty and strong. The physical and moral landscape is firmly, and sometimes even harshly, outlined. It is true that a narrow archipelago cannot have the spaciousness of China, a country with which it is so often contrasted, but those who describe it as being cramped and stunted cannot really know what they are talking about.

We should mistrust, too, the opposite legend which presents us with a "black" Japan instead of a rose-coloured one. About 1930, the literature inspired by Japan in foreign countries switched suddenly from adoration to hatred. According to the indictments published up to 1945, everything Japanese was treacherous, savage and wicked. The real explanation of the tragedy—the fact that millions of docile and too willing people were being exploited and deceived by evil leaders—was often disregarded.

To the list of "Things that Japan is not," we can add a medley of hackneyed and indestructible misconceptions; that the Japanese have yellow complexions, and an inscrutable expression; that their discipline is impeccable and their refinement complete. The Japanese are sometimes called the Prussians of the East. What a mistake! They are secret anarchists, and, in some respects, their artistic unpredictability makes them more like the French. They are said to be fastidious in all things. There is too much bustling and struggling among that overcrowded mass for fastidiousness to appear on the surface.

If I were asked what, in my opinion, is the dominant Japanese characteristic, the one that should be mentioned first and has, so far, been insufficiently stressed, I should say: boisterousness.

How they swarm and rollick! How full of vitality they are and, in the mass, how close to nature! Scores of features in their everyday life suggest a kind of survival of the Middle Ages. This is not to say that Japan does not belong to the twentieth century—the Asiatic twentieth century, no doubt, but one which is contemporary with our own. But even though Japanese life now beats to the rhythm of electric trains, office hours, successive editions of big newspapers and the movements of cinema crowds, there can be felt in it sudden, deep impulses which enable us to understand to some extent what our own Middle Ages must have been like.

The country is rooted in a peasant Japan, which still profoundly conditions the urban crowds. And this peasant Japan, in its turn, still retains something of its ancient, semifeudal structure. Hence its rough solidity; it produces homespun characters, whose pleasures are simple and very soon become noisy, when enjoyed in a group.

Our folklore has disappeared or survives artificially, but Japanese folklore is intensely alive. Its strength can be felt even in the towns, in the street celebrations and temple festivals. It is all-powerful in the countryside, where there are many extraordinary and colourful seasonal celebrations, rarely witnessed by foreigners.

Another manifestation of Japanese boisterousness, for instance, is an incorrigible fondness for taking one's ease, as soon as the polite formalities have been carried out. Good manners do not prevent people tucking up their clothes or lolling full length on mats indoors or partly undressing in the train to be more comfortable when it is hot. It also shows itself in their liking for group life and noisy excursions organized by village, town or factory associations.

The same boisterousness is noticeable in the Rabelaisian side of the Japanese character, when the men are on their own and relaxed. They can make very free with girls and yet, at the same time, remain natural and devoid of viciousness. Popular humour is often crude and evokes peals of hearty laughter.

You will see them in the inns at the warm mountain spas where they are so fond of enjoying themselves for a day or two on the occasion of one or other of the very numerous holidays of the Nipponese calendar. The Sunday banquet will be noisy. When the men go out afterwards to take the air, their faces will be flushed and their steps uncertain, as a result of the copious drafts of *saké* (rice-wine) they have imbibed. The women, for the most part, will have stayed indoors, and any fastidiousness will have remained behind with them. In the evening, the whole party will bathe together with perfect naturalness, frolicking about naked in the scalding steam of the *furo* (Japanese bath). We Westerners have forgotten such simplicity of manners.

The same boisterousness is observable in the "modern nation" side of contemporary Japan, in the ant-hill-like spectacle of the collectivity at work; in the rather disorderly enthusiasm of school-children and students with their passion for learning; in Japanese political life and the newspapers which reflect it; in the noisy elections, the *perpetuum mobile* of the parties and the storms and the comedies of Parliament.

How far removed all this is from the well-mannered, self-controlled Japan that we expected!

But the country is full of contrasts and contradictions. After exploring one aspect of its life, we find that we have been looking at one side of the mountain only; on the opposite slope, the climate is quite different. There is, in fact, another Japan, formal, reserved and difficult of access, the Japan "behind the *shojis*."

The third photograph in this book is a picture of *shojis*. They are the tall, fragile partition-walls of Japanese houses, which shut out the outside world by no more than transparent sheets of paper stretched over a framework of white wood. Shelter barriers they are, yet a whole strange world shelters behind them.

The *shojis* slide open silently in their grooves. In a completely empty room, a man in a silk robe is kneeling, as if at prayer. This is the setting of a very different Japan from the one we have just been discussing. It is the inside of the Japanese home.

But can it be called an "inside" or a "home"? The room is linked to the outside world; it is almost without walls, being open on three sides. The man kneeling there is not shut in at all. It is as if he had been set down in the middle of his garden, on a slightly raised platform and with only a roof to shelter him.

The next room has only one wall; its other sides are made up of these *shojis* or paper screens, arranged as sliding panels. They fit into a larger framework of strong, wooden beams which, with the heavily tiled roof, compose a far less fragile structure than has often been said. But it is a structure built around emptiness. There are no chairs; a Japanese carries his folding-chair with him—in other words, his legs. All he needs for a seat is a silk cushion. There is no furniture except a low table; no sideboards or wardrobes; nothing but built-in cupboards hidden behind sliding panels; no heating; no beds in any of the rooms; no parquet flooring or carpets; the floor is covered with smooth, shiny straw mats, which are walked on only by bare or slippered feet. There are no pictures or knicknacks; no accessories at all, in fact, except two things; a picture painted on a silk roll and hanging perpendicularly on the wall, and a precious vase containing a dead branch and three flowers, arranged with great subtlety.

A sliding panel opens in the far wall of the next room. A servant in a silk kimono appears, carrying a lacquer tray. She had knelt down before opening the panel. She rises, crosses the threshold into the room and kneels again, putting down her tray to make a deep bow. Then she comes to the table and carefully lays upon it the various ingredients of a frugal supper—fish, rice, thin soup and vegetable pickles—which are set out artistically in bowls and saucers of various delicate shapes. Then, walking backwards, she withdraws. With perfect naturalness, she has given a demonstration of an art that we find astonishing, particularly in an ordinary servant—the art of gesture.

At night, the same room serves as a bedroom. The bedding is brought out from a cupboard in the wall; two or three rather thin, silk-covered mattresses are unrolled on the straw mats. The white sheets are hidden beneath brilliant quilted covers whose silk surface is more sumptuously decorated with flowers and birds than the kimono of a princess in a play.

It is the same in a hotel or a middle-class home, in the town or in the country. Behind the *shojis,* which even today do not open easily to admit the European visitor, lies one of the sanctuaries of authentic Japanese life. There we find ourselves in a highly idiomatic setting, consisting not only of white wood, straw mats and paper screens; it includes, in addition, an invisible setting, made up of habits of behaviour, feeling and thought.

However hustled and disturbed by Western civilisation Japan may have been for almost a century now, she remains, basically, the product of something which happened before the modern epoch—of a unique experience undergone, as it were, outside world history. It is as if Japan had belonged to another planet.

After the uncertain dawn of her history, she remained for fifteen centuries a country apart that the world could do without. Had she been entirely non-existent, the fact would have made hardly the slightest difference to the rest of the globe. Her neighbours had only a faint belief in the mysterious isle of Cipango, which was supposed to lie towards the rising sun beyond the storms of the ocean and where, according to the legend, the houses had roofs of gold.

As for Japan herself, she did not quite do without the world. On two occasions before the beginning of the modern age, she was invaded by a foreign culture; in the first place by that of China. Without China, Japan would not be what she is. But whether the influence came from the Chinese or from the Europeans who discovered Japan in the sixteenth century, she remained open to it only for a short time. Incidentally, the invasions were not carried out by enemy soldiers but by ideas that were welcomed as allies. Having taken a great gulp of fresh air, the Japanese shuts himself up again inside his country to assimilate his borrowings from abroad, and to become more intensely Japanese than ever.

The borrowings from China, in particular, were grafted onto a race of people entirely different from the Chinese. The Children of the Rising Sun stamp all the ideas they take from the outside world with their own mark. In the last resort, Japanese culture is essentially and profoundly original.

A proof of originality is that Japan has developed very far along her own individual lines. Other cultures—that of the African Negroes, for instance—have grown up in isolation and achieved a unique form, but they remain rudimentary and primitive. Japan, on the contrary, built up a perfect society, well organized in all its aspects—politics, economics, art, etc.—and marked throughout with the sign of accomplishment—style.

When Europeans rediscovered Japan in the second half of the nineteenth century, their astonishment was equivalent to what they would have felt had they discovered a kingdom in the moon. After that, the tidal wave of Western civilisation washed over the unique world of Japan.

The same thing happened a second time after 1945, for Japan's military adventure had the effect—so great is the tendency of the Japanese to shut themselves in upon themselves—of isolating the country from the rest of the globe.

Twice in less than a century, it was thought that old Japan had been swept away. Twice the West misunderstood—at the time of Meiji's revolution (he was the modern emperor who inaugurated the new age) and after World War II. Many Americans thought Japan had been entirely remodelled, and along American lines.

How naïve an illusion! Can the work of fifteen centuries be destroyed and replaced by something else in the space of a few years? In less than two decades after Hiroshima, it will already be obvious that the Japanese have remained almost untouched.

This is not to say that old Japan survives intact. It certainly does not. The facts are more complex than that. Old Japan can no longer be found in a pure form, just as there will never be a new Japan which is completely cut off from its past. In the Japanese nation, and in the heart of each Japanese, two worlds coexist.

This dichotomy explains some of the conflicts in the Japanese soul. The people themselves, however, manage to put up with it fairly well, being able, luckily, to move constantly and with extreme agility from one aspect of their personality to the other, and having little taste for Cartesian logic.

The Western visitor cannot cope with it so easily. At first all he can see is a horrible mixture. But experience teaches him that to a certain extent a division of attributes has been achieved.

Everything practical and relating to external creativeness usually bears the stamp of the West and constitutes that Westernized Japan which bears witness to the extraordinary Japanese powers of assimilation. But the other side of the picture, the inner side of Japanese thought, the interior of the houses, the innermost parts of the islands and of the countryside, is still Japanese Japan. It is there that one can feel the basic hardness of an

ancient temperament and way of life, which remain stead-
fast or change only with extreme slowness.

That was the side which first attracted the photographer
in his search. When we look at his collection, we see that
at every step he has come across traces of old Japan.

In the houses of Japan, to begin with; every day the
Japanese comes home to find Japan waiting for him. The
businessman who returns from his office by car takes off
his shoes at the entrance to his house and walks barefoot
over the straw mats to doff his suit and slip on a quilted
kimono. He thus rids himself of the Western world and
foreign manners and returns to the habits and rites of old.

The modern girl goes to the University or works as a
typist in a ministry. But here the photographer has caught
her with her stiff silk *obi* (kimono belt) tightly bound
about her waist, arranging flowers in a vase for her
"flower-lesson." After a shopping expedition, a mother
(and sometimes her husband, too) will go to the "tea-
master's" where, with other disciples, she will remain
kneeling for hours to learn the slow discipline of the tea-
ceremonial.

A typical student who works in a laboratory and is a
passionate jazz fan will, when the times comes for him to
take a wife, leave the choice of the girl to his parents,
according to the ancient tradition of obedience. The wedding photograph will show him standing side by side with
a young woman dressed exactly like a figure in an Utamaro
print.

In the towns, the past is still alive in every side street,
in gardens which have been maintained in the old style
for the last three centuries, in the temples where the ordinary folk go to celebrate the feast of one or other of the
thousand Shinto gods or for some festival of the Buddhist
year. Three hundred yards from where the electric train

goes past, carrying its load of manual labourers and office workers to the suburbs, stands the Meiji temple where the photographer has caught a vision, incredibly remote in time, of priests in ancient robes and carrying big paper umbrellas, advancing two by two through the snow among the immense pine trees.

In the theatre, the Middle Ages survive in their entirety; the Kabuki popular classical theatre is spectacular and full of life and colour; the Nô plays, religious dramas intended for the *élite,* are darkened by death and an obsession with the after-life. The fascination that the performances have for many Japanese shows how close the people still are to old Japan, however modern they may be. The Westerner, for his part, can find in the Japanese theatre a still largely unexplored field in which the richest discoveries are yet to be made. The day is not far distant, I am sure, when Western actors and producers will find there unexpected sources of inspiration. In the Nô plays, in particular, with their masked actors, their dances and choruses, one can feel influences which go back to the theatre as it was in the most distant ages of humanity. Such things have been forgotten everywhere else; in Japan, they are still a living force.

Lastly, among the peasants in the countryside, nothing seems to have changed for centuries. There one can discover an immutable Japan, boisterous, vigorous and firmly set in its ancient ways. It is here, too, that the photographer has discovered with delight, far from towns and railways, what is most Japanese in Japan—its natural scenery.

One might almost think that, in Japan, not only the people have been slowly fashioned as in another world, but also the trees, the rocks and the mountains. The trees with their gesticulating branches, the rocks with their curiously tormented shapes, the mountains devoid of pastures, all have a peculiarly unwonted and ancient look. At the same time, everything is bathed in a romantic atmosphere. A hardly perceptible haze simplifies the outlines of the landscape, blurring the fan-like folds of the earth in a series of tones ranging from deep blue to pearly grey. Because of the dampness of the oceanic climate, lush vegetation clothes the shores of the innumerable sea bays with a thick, dark-green growth, among which the trembling bamboos, with their feathery aigrettes, stand out.

How beautiful the rice-fields, which are, according to the season, a mosaic of watery mirrors, a chequered cloak of green and brown, or a great golden carpet! How beautiful the sight of the peasants working there, transplanting each rice-shoot separately in the rain, as if it were a precious flower, and wearing the same grass cloaks as their ancestors in the old prints. The ocean with its myriad isles is never far away, and even in fine weather it is traversed by long, swelling waves set up by distant typhoons.

Japanese scenery, it should be said again, is neither soft nor insipid. The seasons are clear-cut, each with its definite character. Japan has a harsh, wild North, impressive Alps and immense beaches looking onto the Pacific. And the gentler aspects of this strange country can never hide for long its latent violence. The tourist can go nowhere without being reminded of the mysterious fire which seethes beneath the rock. If he is taken to scale a neighbouring mountain, it turns out to be a volcano. If he is invited to bathe in the basement of an inn, he finds that the source of the water is a scalding geyser, which leaps straight from the rock to fall, with a sulphurous smell, into the washing tank. At night, houses move like ships riding at anchor, and the earth trembles. In summer, the sky can be turned topsy-turvy in a few hours by the passing of a typhoon. The frail houses disappear under a protective shell of wooden shutters; but next day, the heavens are again calm and bright.

But, it may be asked, why do you associate the natural setting with old Japan rather than with the modern country? The answer is—and in giving it, we reach beyond photographs and pictures to some of the essential ideas governing the life of the people—that the Japanese, more than any other nation, have been strongly linked, since the most remote times, with the natural scenery surrounding them.

In our countries, modern man has lost contact with nature. He does without nature, and nature no longer influences his life. The Japanese is a child of nature, and in this respect he either will not, or cannot be, modern. Even in the towns, he is so sensitive to the seasons that they affect his everyday life. His complicated household rites vary according to the time of year. At fixed dates, and in obedience to the commands of the lunar calendar, he will eat certain dishes, wear certain clothes, pay certain visits and change the picture hanging on the wall (it is never the same two months running). At the appropriate season, an iris will decorate his house, or again, a chrysanthemum. Family meetings are arranged, as it were, with the maple trees in autumn, the moon of the seventh month or the April cherry trees.

According to whether it is spring or summer, the Japanese change the material of their cushions, screens, lamps or *futons* (the quilted mattresses used for sleeping on); it is as if we were to vary our chairs and other furniture according to the season. A Japanese house seems to dress and undress, to lose, and then recover, its partition-walls. It is so made, moreover, as to form part of the surrounding scenery. In the West, a house is like a block of stone plumped down on the landscape. In Japan, it is open on all sides; it welcomes the landscape into its very heart and brings the garden into its rooms. A temple or an inn, instead of standing out affirmatively against the countryside, is intended to melt and disappear into it.

The personality of the individual dissolves, too. Love of nature, in a Japanese, is really love. It makes him forget himself; his need to admire nature and his thirst to commune with it have a strength unknown in the West. Waves and waterfalls, mountains and clouds afford him keener enjoyment than they do to us—an enjoyment that he cannot do without. His attention is caught not only by some broad prospect, but also by a blade of grass or a single flower, which opens up for him a whole world of delight, or again by a pebble, a curiously shaped root or a piece of old driftwood.

He seems always to have known, even before he left his islands, that there are few countries in the world—none, in any case, in the Far East—where the various aspects of nature are so harmoniously and successfully combined. That is the basis of his patriotism. His affection for his native land is at the root of some of the myths which have so powerfully affected the destiny of his nation—the belief in the divine origin of Japan, and in the uniqueness, among the nations of the world, of the Japanese fatherland with its peculiar mission. The Japanese thought, and thinks, himself different from other men.

In many ways, he *is* different. In the West, various disciplines—Greek humanism, Christian and Jewish mysticism, Roman legalism, the Anglo-Saxon civic sense, etc.—have pruned and trained the instinctive leanings, the spontaneous impulses and the violence of "natural man," as we may term him. Japan, living in a world of its own, remained untouched by these formative influences. What is much more important—the Japanese, with their cult of nature which applies to the animate as well as the inanimate world, were convinced that man must be kept as "natural" as possible and not divorced from his original being, as is the tendency in the West.

Japanese discipline, therefore, does not aim at modifying man and making him into something new but, more simply, at surrounding him with social barriers. His spontaneity, ardour and violence are contained within a system of gestures and rites, but they are still there.

Hence the extreme tensions in the Japanese temperament and the striking contradictions of behaviour. The samurai of old was, no doubt, a knight obedient to a strict code of honour and fidelity, as has often been pointed out; but he was also a formidable creature, capable of throwing off all restraint and changing into a cruel murderer. Until 1945, the modern young Japanese received a Spartan training which developed his aggressive instincts and, at the same time, screwed down over his violent nature a sort of lid of blind obedience and perfect politeness. This made him into an explosive creature, ready to burst like a bomb.

To restrain a nation that had remained more "natural" than Western man, society had to be more formally organised and stricter in the rules it imposed. Everything in Japanese social life is predetermined; improvisation has no place there. According to the situation of the moment, certain gestures must be made, certain rites accomplished, certain words spoken.

Meticulous politeness sets up protective barriers between person and person. Where jealousy and hostility exist, they are repressed and remain unvoiced; speech and attitude may only express esteem and goodwill.

The individual is always part of one setting or another —his family, his trade or profession, his social class, the army, and so on. He is born into a hierarchy, where his exact position is clearly defined. He is always either the inferior or the superior of the person next to him, a debtor or a creditor to whom are due, or who has to pay, certain social debts. The very words he uses express his inferiority or superiority to the person addressed.

Not only is the latent brutality of the "natural man" caught within a network of formalities, so are his feelings for beauty, his sensitivity and his artistic gifts. Few peoples have so keen a liking for artistic creation and enjoyment. But while intensely cultivating this taste for beauty, the Japanese, more than anyone else, have insisted on making it conform to strict canons. It has been disciplined by forms handed down from age to age. There has been imposed upon it a style which forbids any experimental vagaries, but which allows the refined taste to make up in depth for what it loses in extent.

In this respect again, nature dominates the Japanese. Their art pays little attention to human beings; it takes as its subjects leaves and flowers, landscapes, birds, fish and seaweed. The artist is taught to practise self-effacement. Not only does he seek to remove the screen of personality between nature and himself, in order to achieve a better grasp of nature; the pictures resulting from his studies must also remain impersonal. They deal with themes which never change, and conform to a technique which excludes all invention.

Is the result not a stiff and desiccated work of art? We Westerners sometimes think so. But Japanese art is suggestive rather than representative. It employs all sorts of means to incite the spirit to pass far beyond the literal representation contained in the drawing or the painting. To this end, it even uses the cult of the indefinite, and advances to a point bordering on the void. An example of indefiniteness is the blank space left in a picture or the cloud-haze hiding part of a landscape, and which is meant to inspire dreamy contemplation. An example of art verging on the void is the emptiness of the Japanese house, which is meant to facilitate meditation, or to concentrate it more powerfully on the single picture hanging in the alcove.

What is more, the artist perceives in the phenomena of nature, myriads of symbols, to which he holds the key. There exists a language of objects, the secret of which every Japanese learns in childhood. This being so, the narrow picture painted by the artist's brush contains much more than we Westerners can see in its meagre subject. A ripe fruit on an autumn branch or the moon above a waterfall is a window onto a far vaster, invisible world. In the same way as an ideogram contains an idea, so the few strokes of a drawing which represents an object or a landscape can express a message; for instance, joy or sorrow, the transitoriness of the world or its eternal rebirth, and the presence of Buddha behind all things perishable.

Former centuries made the Japanese into a man whose fundamental attitude to life is, in the last resort, that of an artist, an aesthete. He is not a man of principle. The basic law of his social and personal life is not a moral, religious or political law, but an aesthetic one. *The Aesthetic Explanation of Japan* would be a good title for a book that ought to be written some day.

As the Japanese see it, society ought to be a well-built, harmoniously proportioned structure. It is in accordance with a social aesthetic that individuals are placed within a definite framework and taught to discipline their gestures and to adopt pre-determined attitudes in their relations with their family, the state, the Emperor and their ancestors. Order is not only a political necessity; it is an aesthetic imperative. The politeness of its members is one of the factors in the strength of the nation.

It is easy to discern Confucian influence in these ideas. But in Japan, Confucius is not a moralist; the Japanese do not consider morality to be very important. For them, Confucius is not a teacher of the moral law, but a teacher of aesthetics—the aesthetics of human relationships.

Hence it is that the Japanese practise very special techniques of aesthetic training, linking up several forms of activity at once—art, good manners and spiritual development. One such technique is the famous tea-ceremonial. It was invented in China, but the Chinese let it die out again. The Japanese, on the contrary, have carried it to a high pitch of refinement and have kept it alive even in the rush and bustle of modern life.

Kneeling silently as if for a religious service, inside a hall as austere as a chapel, the audience participates raptly in the celebration of a kind of aesthetic mass. The "tea-master" is the officiating priest. The simple action of drinking tea is no more than the pretext for a difficult apprenticeship; the task is to shut out the tumult of the world, to forget the self, to commune with a handful of the initiated in perfect politeness, and above all—this is the supreme object of the tea-ceremonial—to learn, through keen attention to certain simple movements by which a few rare and selected objects are moved from place to place, how to obtain complete mastery of the self in the accomplishment of gestures of absolute purity.

The gospel of the gesture is related to Zen Buddhism, which has given the Japanese the belief that action should be prepared for by meditation. Does this gospel not contain the profound truth that, although passions often determine our gestures, there are at the same time gestures which can silence our passions? And has not the contemplation of beauty, with rapt attention and in forgetfulness of self, the power to eliminate the ugliness of life?

Eliminate ugliness . . . In present-day Japan how can ugliness be avoided? It is rushing in on every side. And with it come the tumult, anxiety and violence of modern life, which cares nothing for harmony and aesthetics. By lingering over a few aspects of the still living past and emphasizing some of its characteristic features (some only, of course; no one could claim to give an account of Japan in a few pages), we may be thought to have wandered too far from actual realities.

Let us leave the frail pavilion where the tea-ceremonial is being celebrated and retrace our steps to the street. What a leap through time! How startling the return to reality! The twentieth century was waiting for us, outside the door of the little house full of peaceful dreaminess.

Modern, startling Japan is mobile and metallic. The Japanese live in wooden houses, but they have built themselves a world of iron and steel, a world of factories, machines and towns (and what towns! An ordinary provincial centre may have more than fifty thousand inhabitants), a world of railways (electric railways and locomotives made in Japan), trams and motor-cars, aerodromes, shipbuilding yards and cinemas.

All the villages are electrified. Pylons carrying the high tension cables stand everywhere in the rice-fields and play leap-frog over the folds of the mountains. Every house has its wireless set, and television is spreading rapidly. The Japanese use the telephone and read newspapers (and what newspapers! The *Asahi* has a circulation of more than five million copies a day). They are building more big shops, they speculate on the Stock Exchange, and they pay income tax; they have limited companies and huge trusts; they produce jet-planes, Olympic champions and atomic physicists.

Japan is a modern state, with political parties and members of Parliament, trade unions, social insurance, a police force supplied with helicopters and a nascent—or renascent—army. Japan is the West in the East. When a European coming from Asia lands there, he discovers that he has already got more than half-way round the globe; he has crossed the meridian beyond which he is no longer moving away from home but, on the contrary, coming back.

One may well wonder how the Japanese have managed to achieve all this, and how they behave in their Westernized Japan.

It is now quite obvious that the Empire of the Rising Sun, because of its centuries of seclusion, had accumulated formidable reserves of energy. Its long sleep was the repose which precedes great effort. Its awakening makes available a fantastic capacity for action, which formerly had been held in check.

Modern Japan is the result of a double explosion, which began at the end of the nineteenth century and is still in progress today. First, an explosion outwards; the Japanese set themselves to master the foreign techniques which they lacked and to seize the territories that might be theirs for the taking. Second, an internal explosion, within the archipelago; its population will have increased fourfold in eighty years, as if the nation's vital energies, too, had suddenly been released and devoted to an increased production of children.

Similarly, the new, modern Japan, reacting against her old immutability, has become extraordinarily changeable. Few countries in the world show such power of rapid transformation. Anyone who leaves Japan for a few months and then goes back again finds it quite different from what it was when he last saw it. It is always building. It consumes new ideas at a surprising rate. A fashion is all the rage for a few months and then gives way to another. Today it is existentialism, tomorrow French songs, the day after strip-tease dancers.

Above all, Japan has a hearty appetite for everything new and foreign, because for so long she was deprived of windows onto the outside world. At a glance, she was able to see, with great lucidity, how sound asleep she had been and how far behind she was. She then conceived a great ambition; she determined to rid herself of everything petty and small; she now aims high, wants to know everything, to know the whole world and to be known by it.

And it so happens that the modern Japanese inherits from his old style of life, however narrow and out-of-date it may have been, certain features which are of the greatest use to him in his metamorphosis. He retains the habit of obedience and his sense of collective discipline; Japan still consists of one head directing millions of limbs.

The frugality of the Japanese citizen is a redoubtable weapon; he puts up with a diet of rice and dried fish and is content to have very little money, in order that the nation may be enriched and strengthened. The tendency to imitate, acquired in a world of tradition, is marvellously useful in the world of invention; it enables him to keep abreast and to adopt foreign techniques without delay. And lastly, he is an indefatigable worker, with a liking for action. He has always given a practical slant to every philosophy, even to Buddhism. He turns out to be the most "Western" of the Asiatics.

Paradoxically enough, he can sometimes allow himself to be even bolder than the European. The latter, even when he forgets his past, is still influenced by it. The Japanese, in his approach to the West, bothers very little about its traditions. He therefore feels himself to be completely free. For instance, if he decides to stop sitting on the floor and to adopt a piece of furniture called a chair, the chair can have any form whatsoever; whatever it is, it will not offend his eye or his ideas. And so he can arrive at Futurism, in one bound. He can create ultra-modern things directly and, at first go, buy the latest thing in tools or works of art.

That is why Europeans belonging to what we call the *avant-garde* are often much more pleased than others when they visit Japan and its ancient civilisation. They discover, for instance, with delight and surprise that the Japanese need make no effort to be at home with Surrealism or abstract art. The Japanese understands and sincerely appreciates Picasso, whereas the Englishman and the American, not to speak of the Frenchman, may be completely baffled.

It is true, on the other hand, that the European visitor has many opportunities of noticing that Western inventions have been badly assimilated. This is the case, especially, in the technical field. The foreigner is often exasperated to see that machines are not well looked after and often do not run smoothly. Modern Japan, like old Japan, is full of contrasts, and there are many shadows as well as bright features.

To begin with, many Japanese behave clumsily when they imitate Western modes of life. Although dignified and impeccable in their traditional kimonos, they often look ill at ease and badly dressed in European suits. In the Japanese setting, their gestures are beautifully controlled; in new surroundings, they can be inharmonious and even brutal. The Japanese ill-treat their engines, put their shoes out of shape and spoil their furniture.

We cannot blame them very much for this; two or three generations are not enough in which to learn how to behave in the world of machines and reinforced concrete. All nations which have recently acquired Western techniques and modes of life are clumsy in the same way. And how heavy-handed we Europeans can be when we venture into Japanese life!

But there is something more unexpected. Observe a Japanese at home, kneeling on his straw mats, in his harmonious, native setting. If a neighbour comes to pay a call, he welcomes him with a thousand courtesies; his manners are perfect, his politeness most refined. But watch the same Japanese on the station platform, when he is getting into the surface or underground train to go to work. He will often push past his neighbour (even the man who was his guest a little while before); he will elbow his way into the compartment and tread on other people's toes without apologizing. This little fact throws considerable light on the attitude of the Japanese towards modern life.

Once he leaves his traditional setting, the Japanese is often at a loss and does not know how to behave; he has not yet learned how to carry over his ancient politeness and acquired gestures from his life into ours. Nor has he learned how to adapt them to changed circumstances.

The reason may be that the deeper significance of what we called the social aesthetic of old Japan had been lost sight of. The art of gesture had gone too far and had often degenerated into a dry formalism. Japanese civilisation had become too exclusively a question of external signs and appearances, in which the politeness which comes from the heart, as well as the dictates of conscience, had been forgotten.

There is also a further cause. When the Japanese approached Western civilisation, they were led astray by an illusion which has done incalculable harm. They made the mistake of supposing that the new world opening up before them was one in which every individual could do what he liked. Once they stepped out of their social framework, they felt themselves free to do without any framework at all.

Compared to the East, the Western world is a world of freedom. The Japanese understood freedom to mean the removal of all rules and restraints. Never having experienced it before, they took to it all the more enthusiastically. But freedom demands a long apprenticeship that they had not undergone, and their lack of experience set them on the road to catastrophe.

The attitude of the individual Japanese, who respects the rules of good behaviour at home but thrusts past his neighbours as soon as he moves into the Westernized and mechanized part of his existence, is a reflection of the attitude of the nation as a whole. When, towards the end of the nineteenth century, the Japanese began to play a part in international politics, they remained perfectly disciplined at home but forgot the rules of good behaviour abroad. They thrust past their neighbours without the slightest compunction. There was no limit to their enterprise and ambition.

The eruption of Japan into the modern world was all the more impetuous since, as we have said, the old tradition aimed at maintaining, unmodified, all the dynamic qualities of natural man. This explains the force and efficiency of Japan's rebirth and also her violence and misdeeds. The appetites and the brutality which, in the old style of life, had been held in check by restraints and respect for social aesthetics, were suddenly free to express themselves in action in the new mode of life.

When the Emperor and the state called upon the subjects of the Rising Sun to throw themselves into this new life, there was a kind of mass exodus of millions of explosive individuals. As was natural, the military caste gradually came to the top, because it was they who had systematically conditioned the youth of the nation to be absolutely disciplined on the surface and violent underneath.

This led first to Pearl Harbour, then later to Hiroshima . . . See the tragic picture of the legless man, playing the mandolin to earn his keep.

And so we come to the photographs of present-day Japan. They show a country which, after a catastrophic defeat, displayed extraordinary energy in clearing away the ruins and rebuilding. A hundred towns had to be reconstructed, factories and trade had to be set going again, the whole political structure of the country had to be overhauled. But Japan, deprived of her territorial conquests, is no longer the "Great Japan" of yesterday. Denying the whole course of her history, she attempted a spectacular aggression from her narrow archipelago; as a result, she is confined there once again, she has been brought back to her starting point, to the exiguous space she occupied in the early part of the reign of the Emperor Meiji.

As was the case then, one of her most serious problems is how to catch up with other nations in the modern world without, at the same time, allowing her ancient civilisation to perish. Now more than ever before, Japan is torn between the longing for nourishment from abroad and the old instinct prompting her to remain faithful to her traditions.

How strong those traditions still are can be seen as soon as we try to gauge how far Japan has been Americanized since the end of the war. No one acquainted with the facts of the case could be deceived by appearances into thinking that the American occupation has permanently modified Japanese life.

The Japanese, from behind their *shojis*, have observed

the Americans. They have decided there is little they can learn from them except technical skills, and that the American way of life is not for the Japanese. They remain attached to the emptiness and absence of comfort of their furnitureless, unheated homes, their *tatamis* (straw mats), and their bowls of rice and chopsticks, not only because an Americanized life would be too costly for them, but also because frugality is in their very blood; any self-respecting Japanese despises luxury and money.

The democracy they learned—or re-learned—from Mac-Arthur was quickly revised and corrected according to Japanese notions. No doubt, the Emperor has lost his semidivine character, but his authority has not diminished—far from it—since it has been founded on affection instead of fear. Japanese women have the vote, often wear dresses instead of kimonos and are freer than before, at least in the towns, but generally speaking the husband is still lord and master in the home, particularly in the country districts. The parliamentary system works, but it is not very different from what it was before the beginning of the military era.

The Americans have been quite unable to rid the Japanese of the habit, inherited from feudal times, of giving and acknowledging the innumerable obeisances which mark the degrees in the social hierarchy. And if there is one field in which Japan has made an effort to return to the past, it is with regard to politeness, at least when "behind the *shojis*."

Yet it is unthinkable that the Country of the Rising Sun should ever return to its old isolation. It can never again become the "kingdom in the moon" that it once was. And paradoxically enough, it is because defeat has again shut the Japanese within their islands that they are obliged to develop their relations with the outside world as much as possible.

Japan has ninety-five million inhabitants in an area which is four-fifths that of France. Before the last quarter of the century, the population will be a hundred million, and the birth rate will still be rising. A hundred million people will have to live on four islands! They will, inevitably, be poor. And above all, they will be more dependent than ever on trade with foreign countries. To feed all these millions, foodstuffs will have to be imported; to give them employment, new industries must be developed in the towns and the countryside; and to keep her factories going, Japan, now without an Empire, will be completely dependent on foreign countries for purchases of raw materials and sales of manufactured goods. She will be one of the countries most sensitive to the fluctuations of world economy, one of those most likely to suffer from disturbances in the international situation.

Already the Japanese are finding that it is difficult to breathe; that fresh air from the outside world is not arriving as quickly as it should. Japan's trade with abroad is recovering with difficulty, because it is meeting with Western competition. Communist markets are closed to it. The Japanese are wondering anxiously if they will be able, as they so ardently desire, to win a place among the free nations, and what chance they have of keeping it, if they get it.

We, for our part, should ask ourselves what would happen if, through selfishness or indifference, we made the Western community of nations "unlivable-in" for the new post-war Japan. We might well see her change sides in order to survive. In spite of her profoundly anti-Russian and anti-Communist instincts, she might resign herself to joining up with China and the U.S.S.R. After the first tidal wave of the Meiji revolution and second one of the post-war era, we might see a third—the Marxist tidal wave —come from abroad and engulf the country. What upheavals it could cause in everything that has remained, until now, so obstinately Japanese!

These fears are not inspired by political passion. I have tried to forget politics altogether in writing these few pages. On the contrary, I am anxious that Japan should be spared those political disturbances which have done her such harm in the past.

Japan needs Western aid in order to live and prosper in peace, so that material difficulties do not incite her to further military adventures. At the same time, the Western nations need Japan, not to use her as a weapon in their quarrels by reawakening the violence in her nature, but for the contribution she can make to modern humanism, thanks to the very individual artistic and spiritual values she has evolved throughout her long history.

It is in the interests of us all that Japan should remain faithful to her old virtues and allow us to become acquainted with them. She must be able to get to know us, and we to get to know her. It would be disastrous both for herself and for us if she were again shut off from us by politics and were to be hidden by the iron curtain which already conceals part of Asia.

We need the smile of Japan and her politeness. We do not want her to return to grimacing militarism and totalitarianism. Let us pray that she will never again be visited by the appalling flash of the atomic bomb; if she were, some of the world's most ancient treasures of art would be destroyed, along with the teeming multitudes of one of the most interesting peoples in the world.

The tragedy of Japan is that its most profoundly original features are fragile and are threatened by the storms of the future. This very fragility should make us more sympathetic towards her. It makes even more precious any knowledge we can acquire of the strange world shown in these photographs.   (Translated by J. G. Weightman)

OLD JAPAN

2 In the Ryoanji, a Kyoto temple. The priest, overcome by the heat, has fallen asleep on his knees. The *shojis* having been opened on the side facing the courtyard, the sun shines into the old house.

3 Behind this *shoji,* or window, the Japanese live their family life. The panes are not made of glass but of white paper. If one of them gets torn, a new piece of paper is glued in. New white panes and older yellowing ones mingle in a picturesque pattern. The window slides in a groove in the wooden frame.

4 The Silver Pavilion at Kyoto. It was built towards the end of the fifteenth century by a statesman who used it as a resting-place after the fatigues of war. It became one of the cradles of the tea-ceremonial and of the art of gardening.

5 The iris, whose leaf is as keen as a samurai's blade, signifies strength. The Japanese have a symbolic flower-language. On the occasion of the Boys' Festival, they bathe their sons in iris water, to make them healthy.

6 The lotus is the symbol of purity, because it rises from the muddy bottom of the pond to spread its leaves above the surface of the water and to offer up to the heavens a wonderful pink flower. It is the plant of Buddha; he is represented as sitting in the centre of a full-blown lotus-flower.

4

7 Schoolgirls contemplating a temple garden at the Silver Pavilion at Kyoto.

8 A mound of white sand, sparkling among the pines in the garden of the Silver Pavilion. It, too, is meant to appeal to the imagination when seen at night, gleaming palely in the light of the moon.

9 A famous Kyoto garden. It has remained unchanged since it was first laid out, about 1450. The white sand is carefully raked, and the strange old stones are placed in twos, threes and fives. Various interpretations of its meaning have been suggested and – who knows? – all may be correct or incorrect. It is an esoteric garden which invites the visitor to dreamy meditation on the mystery and poetry of the external world.

10 The house of the painter Hashimoto Kwansetsu, in Tokyo. The tea-pavilion in the garden is a sign of Chinese influence; Hashimoto Kwansetsu had visited China.

11 Old stone lanterns are placed at intervals along the path leading to the tea-pavilions in the gardens of Katsura Palace. Oil-lamps can be lit inside them at night. These lanterns were once used to light the temple approaches; later they were placed in the gardens more as ornaments than as a means of illumination.

12 Stepping-stones in the iris pond at Kyoto – a dotted line leading into the secrets of old Japan.

13
14 Priests of the modern Meiji Temple, which was built in
honour of the emperor who opened up Japan to Western
influence. Wearing ancient robes and headdresses, they
have been to open the temple-gates to members of the
Imperial Family, who are to be honoured on the occasion
of Meiji's anniversary celebrations.

15 Japanese schools are modern yet they keep the old traditions alive. Letterwriting (calligraphy) and drawing are most important. In summertime pupils are seen all over gardens and shrines with their sketchbooks. Girl watching a boy painting at Heian-Shrine in Kyoto.

16 A trough of running water stands at the entrance of every temple, so that pilgrims can carry out their symbolic ablutions, cleanliness being the first commandment of the Shinto religion. These school-children are rinsing out their mouths and washing their hands, while at the same time satisfying their thirst.

17 Elsewhere, as at the Kiyomizu Temple in Kyoto, there are baths in which the faithful, to do penance, stand – sometimes naked – under a shower of icy water.

18 Pilgrims at the Yasukuni Temple in Tokyo. These anxious-faced watchers have come to ''meet'' their sons, brothers or husbands, who were killed in the war. The Japanese believe that the souls of the slain dwell in this temple and watch over the Fatherland. The steps are littered with paper money contributed by the pilgrims towards the upkeep of the temple.

19 Women worshippers who have been to pray in a Buddhist temple. Many temples are places where people go to relax as well as to worship, and green tea is served there, free of charge. Old women may spend the day there with their grandchildren.

20 The Kitano Temple at Kyoto is dedicated to Michizane Sugawara, the faithful minister of one of the early emperors. Having been sentenced to exile because of a false accusation, he fled on a bull's back. The peasant in the photograph believes that the statue of the bull radiates a supernatural force.

21 The Imperial Palace Grounds in Tokyo are now open to the public. A romantic youth enjoys his violin on the grass.

22 An old man praying in front of images of Jizo Bosatsu, the children's Buddha. Pieces of children's clothing are tied round the necks of the little statues. Parents who have an ailing child take one of these pieces of clothing and place it under the child's pillow, to act as a talisman.

23 Lotus leaves in a pond at the moss-garden in Kyoto. The midday sun sparkling on the water produces a reddish reflection because of the muddy bottom.

24 Hundreds of twisted pieces of paper fastened by pilgrims to the wooden gate of a temple. They are letters addressed to the Gods – secret prayers, often offered up by lovers asking for divine help.

25 The impressive Todaiji Temple at Nara shelters a giant statue of the great Buddha. Groups of students and school-children come from all parts of Japan to visit the old capital of Nara with its art treasures.

26 On entering a temple (as here) or a private house, the Japanese leave their shoes on the threshold and walk over the polished wood floor or straw mats barefoot or in socks or stockings. Inscriptions painted on screens greet the visitor to this temple.

27 The Great Buddha of Nara, an enormous bronze statue, which has stood here since its erection in the year 749. It is more than forty-five feet high and must weigh about 500 tons. Even if the art of casting bronze were to be rediscovered, would it be possible, today, to recapture the faith of the period which saw the creation of this powerful monument?

28 Part of the Imperial Katsura Palace, near Kyoto, a famous work of Japanese architecture. Built at the beginning of the 17th century it is still a source for modern designers.

29 Girl students and young office-workers visiting a flower exhibition. They have stopped to watch an expert arranging flowers in a vase.

30 The arranging of flowers has been raised to the status of an art requiring long and strenuous study. There are rarely more than three blooms to a vase, but minute rules govern the composition of the bunch, the choice of the vase, the way the stems point, and so on. In addition to these rules, there is a ''philosophy of flowers,'' which claims to combine the active and passive principles in nature, in accordance with the jealously guarded traditions of the various schools of practitioners of this graceful art.

31 An old, sunken boat slowly mouldering away in a pond in the moss-garden at Kyoto. The mystery of reflections and shadows on water and leaves is a subject dear to the hearts of Japanese painters. The photographer, too, manages to express it.

32 A fragment of an old poem, engraved on a stone column in a garden. Such unexpected snatches of beauty can be discovered at every step in the old town of Kyoto. The foreign visitor cannot always understand their meaning, but he is moved by their close harmony with the surrounding scenery.

33 Bamboo in another of the many exquisite large gardens in Kyoto, a treasury of the finest in Japanese landscapes.

34 A Buddha, standing forgotten among damp creepers, is visited by a snail. This was the garden of Hashimoto, a painter of the old school, who died many years ago. He was very fond of it; his son studied painting in Paris and went over to the ''moderns,'' so the garden is left to run wild.

35 Pilgrims at Mount Hiei, the Buddhist holy mountain near Kyoto. They are dressed in costumes identical with those worn by pilgrims in the old days, and they hope that by climbing tirelessly up and down the mountain paths from temple to temple they will earn the right of entry to the Buddhist paradise.

36 A mirror, a divine symbol on Shinto altars, is here being prayed to by a Buddhist pilgrim at the Kyomizu Temple. Buddhism and Shintoism are often allied. Many Japanese born into the Shinto religion, and who have never practised any other, decide to become Buddhists before they die.

34

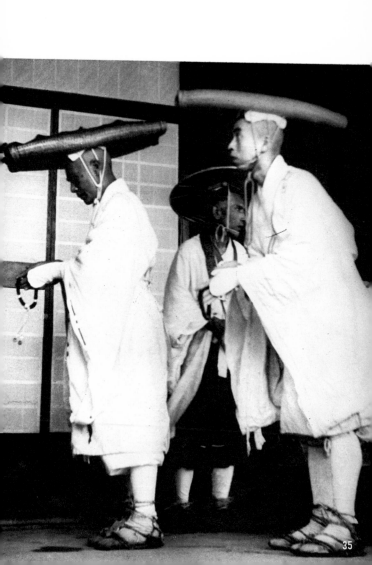

37 A statue of a demon, dating from the seventh century and which keeps watch in front of the Great Buddha of Nara. At temple entrances, there are often two frightening demons, one open-mouthed, the other with its mouth shut.

38 In the course of the tea-ceremony, the tea-master places the bamboo ladle on the pot of boiling water in a perfectly stylised, traditional gesture. The officiating tea-master, here, is Sen Shochitsu, a modern successor of Rikyu, the great fifteenth century tea-master. In ordinary circumstances, of course, tea is drunk without ceremony.

39 ''There is no secret in the art of the tea-ceremonial,'' Rikyu used to say. ''What does it consist of? Simply this: you boil the water, then you make the tea, and then you drink it according to the traditional rules. That is all there is to know.'' ''I know how to do all that already,'' someone said. ''If there really is someone who knows how to do it,'' answered the master, ''I will become his pupil.''

40 The art of flower-arranging, like the tea-ceremonial, is one of the accomplishments of any well-brought-up young lady. Both help to sharpen the aesthetic sense and give training in gesture and taste. At the same time, they are methods of relaxation and, as such, valuable to the Japanese in the bustle of modern life.

41 The *tokonoma* is an alcove in the main room of the house, devoted to the displaying of a painting – often a roll of ornamental writing – and a bunch of flowers. The choice and arrangement of both are attended to with great care, as can be seen from the attitude of this connoisseur who has put himself in a crouching position to get a better view of the effect produced.

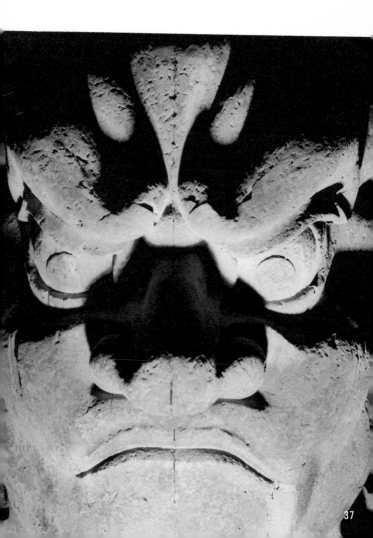

42 For her wedding, the modern girl is obliged to hire a wig to get the high-piled effect of the traditional hair-style. The head is adorned with tortoise-shell combs on the tips of which are inscribed characters – "Fir-tree, bamboo and plum-tree" – with a symbolic significance. Who could guess that the young bride shown here in the heavy traditional wedding kimono and wearing a white head-band (it is supposed to prevent the growth of horns of jealousy) is a shorthand typist in one of the big Tokyo stores?

43 In three red lacquer cups, which are exchanged three times, the bride and bridegroom solemnly drink the very light rice-wine called *saké;* having done this, they are married. Even if the young woman normally dresses in the European fashion, she wears a ceremonial kimono on her wedding-day. But the bridegroom wears a morning-coat.

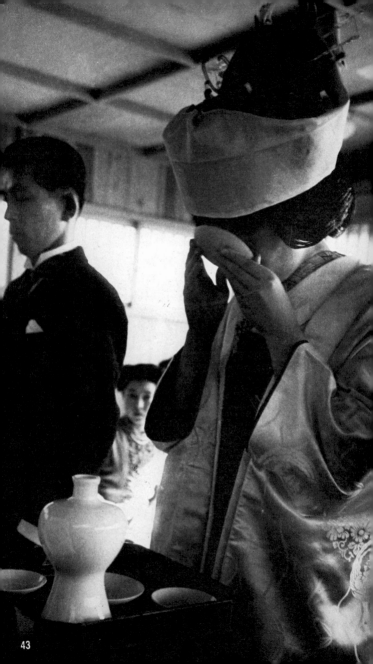

JAPAN TODAY

44

44 The Emperor Hirohito leaving Tokyo by train, with the Empress. As the train moves off, a minister who had formed part of the escort – along with the station-master and everyone else present – bows bareheaded to the Imperial carriage, on which can be seen the badge of the gold chrysanthemum.

45 The Imperial couple are both dressed in European clothes, but she walks behind him, according to ancient custom. Only the Imperial escort and journalists are allowed onto the platform, where a red carpet has been laid down. Suburban traffic continues at the opposite platform.

46 The whole attitude and bearing of this railway employee supervising the platform arrangements is expressive of the discipline and sense of duty of the Japanese official in uniform.

47 Although the Imperial limousine is an out-of-date model, it excites almost as much astonishment in the younger generation as the presence of the Emperor himself.

48 School-children of Hiroshima, impatiently awaiting the arrival of the Emperor, who is due to arrive on his first visit to the town since the end of the war. "Is that him?", one of them is wondering, with the curiosity of a little post-war Japanese, in whom familiarity is still tempered with something of the old awe. The flags will wave to the thrice-repeated cry of "Banzai" ("ten thousand years of happiness").

49 A survivor of the atomic bomb explosion at Hiroshima. He tried to take shelter in the doorway of a house three miles from the centre of the explosion, but the radioactive rays covered him with burns, and his right hand has been paralysed ever since.

50 The bomb fell near this building, a former exhibition hall. Its metal and reinforced concrete framework withstood the blast, but everything in the vicinity was obliterated. A flourishing trade in relics and souvenirs is now carried on at wooden stalls near the tombstones and inscriptions which proclaim: "Let there be no more Hiroshimas!"

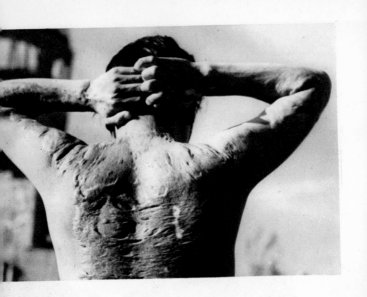

50

51 Motor traffic in Tokyo is heavy and noisy. ''Keep right,'' says the inscription in Japanese and English. Only cars going to the Imperial Palace turn left; the Palace Gates are quite near.

52 A pedestrian crossing at Ginza, in the heart of the capital.

53 Kimonos are rarely worn now on ordinary occasions. In one of the big stores a housewife wearing a kimono chooses a European dress in the ready-made department.

54 There are no beggars in Japanese towns, but since the defeat, poverty has often been apparent among the lower classes. The bombs destroyed more than a hundred towns.

55 The Japanese eat frugally at home. There is a gulf between the two generations shown here, as can be seen by their clothes and attitudes. But family solidarity remains firmly rooted, and the young have a great respect for the old. Elderly parents usually live in with their married children.

56 Paper flowers which unfold when put into water are a pleasing gift for children, in addition to the innumerable mechanical toys which are manufactured in Tokyo. Children play an important part in Japanese life, and they live in a paradise of cheap toys.

ONLY
TURN
RIGHT

51

57 Tokyo's streets are ever-changing – steel structures tower over small houses, offices are being built. The trade and business center of the capital is almost identical with that of any large European city.

58 Cheap *kakemonos* (paintings on rolls of silk). These are the Tokyo equivalents of the ''cheap daubs'' sold in Europe. The painting of Christ is explained by the curiosity, not to say fascination, aroused by Christianity during the spiritual uncertainty of the post-war period.

59 This little girl is earning her living as a flower-seller, after school-hours. Defeat and the American occupation have caused many upheavals in Japanese life. To help the family budget, children sell flowers very late in the evening at night-club doors. They are bought by American soldiers who give them to their girls.

60 Strip-tease dancers in their music-hall dressing-room. Strip-tease dancing was imported from America and has been all the rage since the occupation. It is occasionally given a Japanese flavour by being fitted into some scene taken from the feudal period. It calls for little talent on the part of the dancer and can be very profitable.

61 A woman from the country takes a break from selling sweets to have her lunch. The fair is on at the annual festival of the bull, the sacred animal of the Kitano Temple in Kyoto, a gay and colorful event.

62 A boy watches from his houseboat window the traffic on the Sumida River in Tokyo. His family, like many others, lives and earns its living on the water.

63 A lantern-maker's shop at Kyoto. Handicrafts are losing ground through the development of industry, and small shopkeepers now have to contend with competition from the big stores. Small workshops are still numerous, however, in the poorer districts.

64 The Picasso exhibition at Tokyo. Not only do the Japanese appreciate their own traditional art; they are often very enthusiastic, too, about Western art, even when it is "avant-garde." The Picasso and Matisse exhibitions, both of which visited several towns, were seen by more than three million people.

65 A Japanese student. In shrunken, post-war Japan, there is a surplus of University graduates; many of them have to be content to earn their living as lift-attendants or waiters.

66 A legless ex-serviceman, begging in the Asakusa district in Tokyo. Many soldiers wounded in the last war are reduced to such extremities, because the government does not allow them a pension.

67 An American soldier, just back from Korea, hopes to become acquainted with the strip-tease dancers by taking them cigarettes and chocolate.

68 Boys and girls watch a picture "Punch and Judy" show. The professional story-teller, who also carries bottles of sweets, sets up his stand on the luggage-carrier of his bicycle at a street-corner.

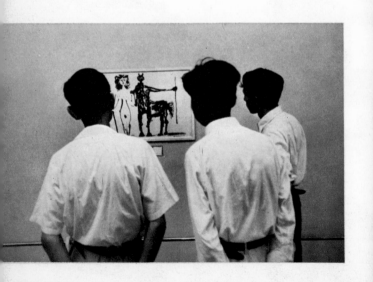

69 In the "town of a hundred millions" (Tokyo), a great many poverty-stricken water-men and bargees live in barges and sampans along the river Sumida.

70 There is practically no illiteracy in Japan. People read enthusiastically even in book shops and department stores – everything from the newest novels to comics.

71 A countrywoman, reading the newspapers on her doorstep. The further one moves from the capital, the weaker Western influence becomes. The woman here is in her working-clothes – a *mompei*, a sort of kimono-cum-trousers.

72 A rag-man reads the newspaper outside the office of a big daily. The men keep in touch with events by means of the press and the radio.

73 Long pieces of silk drying in the wind above the river-bed near Kyoto, the centre of the silk industry. They have been washed in running water to remove excess dye.

74 A bicycle coolie has a nap on Tokyo's busiest street, the Ginza. He will be alert and ready to work in an instant on hearing the call ''coolie.''

75 A worker in an engineering factory. Since the end of the war, the equipment in many factories has become out-of-date.

76 Working conditions often remain very primitive. In this rolling-mill the worker's only protection from the heat given off by the hot sheets of metal is a wet towel tied around his face.

77 The poorer districts of the town border on the rice-fields and suffer from their dampness. In winter, the snow-covered rice-fields are a dismal bog, spiky with broken lotus stems.

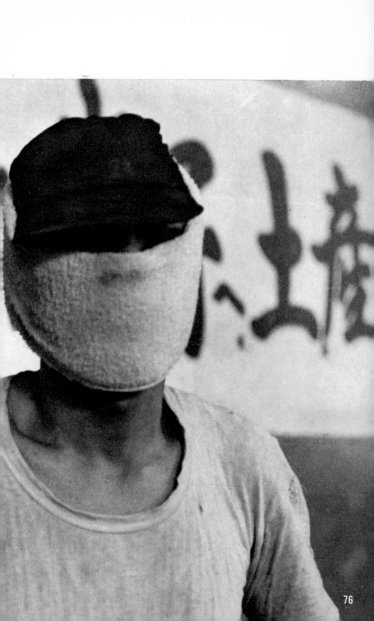

78 A peasant woman at work. In spring, life returns to the rice-fields, and the peasants carefully rebuild the innumerable little earth banks of the canals carrying the water needed by the rice-plants.

79 An umbrella drying in the sun. The old, country umbrella is made of oiled paper. It is still used quite frequently in the towns by women wearing kimonos and by geishas. It is a delightful, brightly-coloured object, decorated with a pattern of flowers.

80 Peasants busy in the fields below Mount Fuji. Agricultural work is often carried on with very primitive instruments, such as this cow-drawn plough.

81 A winter landscape. All the available land is cultivated, right up to the mountain slopes. The mist, shot through with sunlight, composes a landscape recalling a tinted drawing by one of the old masters.

82 Fujiyama rears its snowy head above the rice-field where the harvest has been gathered in. Mount Fuji has always fascinated the Japanese as the symbol of a whole ideal of strength, purity and harmony. Its base is almost at sea-level, and the peak reaches 12,365 feet. It is an extinct volcano; the last eruption was in 1707. It is considered as a holy mountain, and thousands of pilgrims climb it every summer.

83 A mother carries her baby tied to her back and protected in winter by a thick kimono or blanket. This arrangement allows her to go about her work, without having to leave the baby in anyone else's charge.

84 A little girl with a cat. Japanese cats are tail-less. It used to be thought that the few cats with long tails were magic animals, who could change themselves into all sorts of malevolent creatures.

85 An old countrywoman, with Mount Fuji in the background. Notice the layers of kimono which protect her against the cold. Japanese peasants are an abstemious and hardy race. The women work in the fields to an advanced age.

86 This little girl, in Chinese-style trousers and a Japanese schoolgirl jacket, is carrying a drum on her tricycle to announce the arrival of itinerant salesmen.

87 A perambulator, made of bamboo basket-work. There are not many of them, since mothers usually prefer to carry their children in their arms or on their backs.

88 The younger generation goes in enthusiastically for physical training. Modern games such as volleyball and baseball, although very popular, have not eliminated traditional Japanese sports such as *judo*, or fencing with sticks.

89 *Banzai* for the Emperor! On the occasion of a visit to the provinces by the Sovereign, school-children show that the young Japanese have not lost their respect for the Emperor, even if he is no longer considered as a demi-god.

90 A *sumo* champion, with his hair arranged in the traditional style, scatters a handful of salt on the floor, as a purification rite before the beginning of a match. *Sumo*, a very ancient form of wrestling, is practiced by giants who are specially fattened up for the purpose. It is the favorite sport of the masses.

THE TRADITIONAL
JAPANESE THEATRE

91

91 Bongoro, a deaf and half-blind puppet expert, waits to go on with his puppet. It is a curious paradox that the gestures and theatrical style of these marionettes should have had such a strong influence on the style of the live actors of the classical theatre.

92 The puppet and his manipulator have become almost one and the same person. To excel in this very specialised art, more than twenty years' training is needed.

93 The manipulator of the puppet appears on the stage with it. Its attitudes and gestures are so life-like that after a few minutes the audience notice only it and forget about the person to whom it owes its being.

94 At the Osaka puppet theatre, which dates from the end of the eighteenth century. The puppets with their complicated mechanism and precious costumes are made in the theatre's own workshops.

95 A child's doll, representing a princess of old Japan. Such classical dolls are not so much playthings as works of art. They are rarely handled by the little girls to whom they belong, but are usually kept in glass cases. A doll often represents, as this one does, a character in the Kabuki or the Nô plays.

96 Behind the scenes, the singer who sings and recites on behalf of the marionettes, receives a visitor. Bowing low over the straw mats, according to the rules of Japanese politeness, he offers his visiting-card and will receive the other person's in exchange. This is the way in which introductions are made.

97 A Kabuki actor patiently awaits his entrance backstage.

98 An actor making up as a woman. The female parts are played by men. The Kabuki theatre was developed in the sixteenth century, and the action of the plays is normally set in feudal Japan. The actors are accompanied by an orchestra of *shamisen*-players (the shamisen is a three-stringed mandolin) and by singers.

99 At the Kabuki theatre, the actor Bondo Mitsugoro prays in front of a little altar in his dressing-room before going onto the stage. The Kabuki plays are popular classical dramas. The sets are extremely ornate, and a revolving stage allows rapid changes of scenery.

100 Mitsugoro, one of the most famous Kabuki actors, has applied his face make-up and is beginning the long and arduous dressing in costume.

101 Now he is helped on with the heavy costume of a mediaeval hero. His make-up is almost like a mask.

102 Clad in armour, and wearing a kimono of extraordinary richness, the seventy-seven year old Mitsugoro is sitting on a stool in his dressing-room, waiting to go on to play the part of ''Yanoné.''

103 The chorus of the Nô theatre. The Nô plays are aristocratic and religious works of Buddhist inspiration, intended almost entirely for the *élite*. Here again the female parts are played by men. The performers are unpaid and act in these plays for the love of the thing.

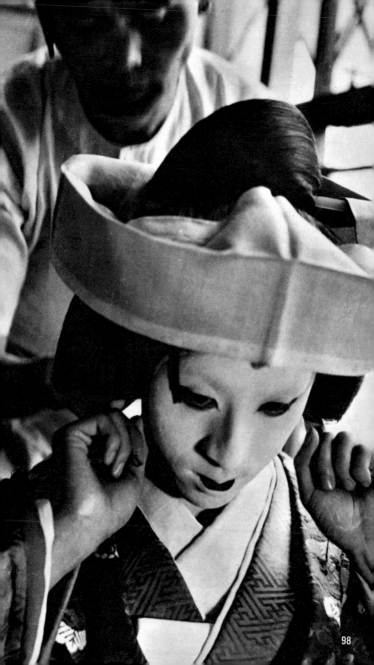

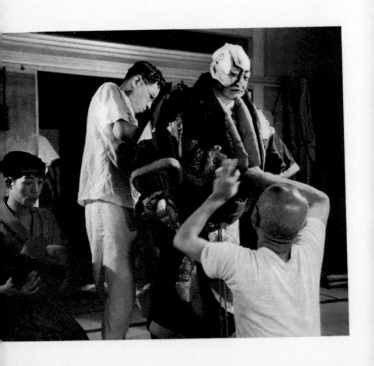

104 The dance of the Heavenly Fairy in the Nô play entitled "The Feather Robe." This is an open-air performance, and part of the annual celebrations in honour of the memory of the Emperor Meiji.

105 Unlike the actors of the Kabuki theatre, the Nô players are masked. The masks are very precious works of art made by famous craftsmen and are handed down from generation to generation. This mask represents a girl or a fairy. The Nô plays are performed without any scenery on a square stage in in the middle of the auditorium. There are only two or three characters. The extraordinarily sumptuous costumes are in sharp contrast to the bareness of the setting.

106 The dance is the climax of the drama. It is performed to the sound of tambourines and a flute. The chorus intervenes from time to time with its strangely poignant chant. The dancer hardly lifts his feet from the ground and seems to slide miraculously over the smooth, mirror-like stage.

107 The Bugaku dances were, for a long time, reserved exclusively for the Imperial Court, and ordinary people were not allowed to see them. The very rich brocade costumes are an inheritance of the ancient Asiatic folklore of more than two thousand years ago. These actors belong to a company which has been formed to revive the splendours of this ancient art and to present it to the general public, if not regularly at least several times a year.

108 A flute-player for the Bugaku dances. These are ancient dances of Asiatic origin, which were kept alive in Japan for the entertainment of the Emperor and his Court after they had died out in their country of origin, which was usually Korea or China.

109 The Gagaku orchestra, which plays the ancient music to accompany the Bugaku dances. It includes, in addition to the *koto* and the *biwa* (varieties of the harp and the lute), the *sho*, a wind instrument, a little bamboo organ with fourteen reeds.

110 A great drum beats time to steps and gestures which have not changed since the most distant ages. The drum is marked with the magical sign, or *tomoye*, which symbolizes the movement of the elements in a state of perpetual becoming.

WERNER
BISCHOF

In 1949 Werner Bischof was a man who found himself somewhat alone in Zurich, although he knew everyone and had deep and devoted friendships.

He knew he must leave. His experience with the Swiss Red Cross in Eastern Europe had given him a sense of photographic mission, and he was determined to go beyond the tidy world of Switzerland and to use the power of his camera to reveal mankind.

He could have been a staff photographer on one of the great picture magazines. But the discipline of staff work was not for him. His discipline was his own—and far stricter than that of any staff. He could only work happily as his own master. And so, after a brief but friendly relationship with one of the commercial picture agencies, he found it natural to associate himself, in 1949, with the photographers of "Magnum"—men who were also their own masters because "Magnum" had been founded as a photographers' cooperative by men whom Werner Bischof respected: Robert Capa and Henri Cartier-Bresson and David ("Chim") Seymour and George Rodger.

Almost simultaneously, Werner and his friend Ernst Haas of Vienna joined the "Magnum" group in Paris. The dream was on, and at times it was a nightmare. "Magnum" had little money and a tiny staff, and editors were not always buying the stories as "Magnum" photographers saw them. Many times "Magnum" appeared to magnify, rather than diminish, the individual problems of its members.

But in "Magnum" there was a common cause and there was the visionary Capa to see it through the rough spots. No two men were more unlike than Capa and Werner, and yet they loved each other as brothers. Each was spared the great pain which knowledge of the other's sudden death would have caused.

Beyond brotherhood "Magnum" gave to Werner a range of experience he could not have otherwise obtained. It took him first to Italy and England and Scotland, on a variety of assignments where he first practiced "photo-journalism." Then it took him to Japan, where he did some of his greatest work, embracing both the subtle beauty of Japanese art (which Werner caught perhaps more successfully than any Westerner has ever done) and also the suffering and the confusion of a people living with a 5th century Emperor and a 20th century atomic bomb.

And to Korea, where he photographed the shattering effects of war upon its children. And to Indo-China, where he photographed the uncertain war itself, and went beyond it to a village untouched by war. And to India, where he saw and photographed the death mask of famine upon living people.

Throughout these travels he photographed in his own

way, which "Magnum" did not change, except that he became more conscious of journalism. His style remained as ever—a style which defied analysis because its only weakness was perhaps its very perfection. Finally he came to America, and at first was miserable in its air-conditioned civilization until again he came to know the people and to sense and photograph the power of the great cities.

In New York he bought a jeep, and with his wife set out for South America. In Mexico they had to part. He flew to assignments in Chile and Peru and wrote: "Winter is coming here and life is sad. It is no comparison to the Far East and I am sure not to stay here longer than I must." A few days later, high in the Andes, the length of his stay was determined forever.

In the Paris and New York offices of "Magnum" there now hang small bronze plaques which read: "In Memory of Robert Capa and Werner Bischof—May Magnum Live Always in the Spirit They Gave It."

—John G. Morris, Executive Editor, Magnum

BISCHOF — A CHRONOLOGY

1916 — Born in Zurich, Switzerland

1922 — Lower schools in Waldshut, Germany

1931 — College in Schiers, Switzerland

1932 — School for Arts and Crafts, Zurich

1936 — Graduation, military service, free-lance work

1938 — Collaborates as graphic designer for "Graphis"

1939 — Works for National Exhibition of Switzerland, in Paris to paint, military service

1942 — Published in "Du" magazine, becomes staff member

1944 — Special issue "Du," first reportage on infirm youth

1945 — Works for "Du" in post-war France, Germany, Holland

1946 — In Italy and Greece for "Swiss Relief"

1947 — Travels through Hungary and Rumania

1948 — Covers St. Moritz Olympics for "Life," second trip to Eastern Europe results in special issue "Du"

1949 — Marries, works in England with "Picture Post" and "Observer," joins "Magnum"

1950 — Birth of his first son, travels to Italy, France

1951 — "Life" assignment in India, expedition along Tibetan border, flies to Tokyo

1952 — Korea, Japan, Hong Kong, Indo-China

1953 — Special issue "Du" on Far East, prepares JAPAN, covers Coronation for "Life," comes to U.S.

1954 — Mexico, Panama, Chile, Peru, Amazon river trip. Automobile accident May 16th. Second son born May 25th.